Oscar's Opposites

by Sam Godwin

MACDONALD YOUNG BOOKS

Today is Oscar's birthday.

I wonder what his birthday present will be.

'Is it a **big** present or a **small** present?' Oscar asks his brother Stan.

6

'Is it a **tall** present or a **short** present?' Oscar asks his sister Suzy.

9

'Will I use my present when it's **hot** or when it's **cold**?' Oscar asks his mum.

11

'Is it a **soft** present or a **hard** present?' Oscar asks his dad.

13

'Will I use my present when it's **wet** or **dry**?' Oscar asks his cousin Molly.

'Is it a **heavy** present or a **light** present?' Oscar asks his granny.

What can the presents be?

Big

Small

Tall

Short

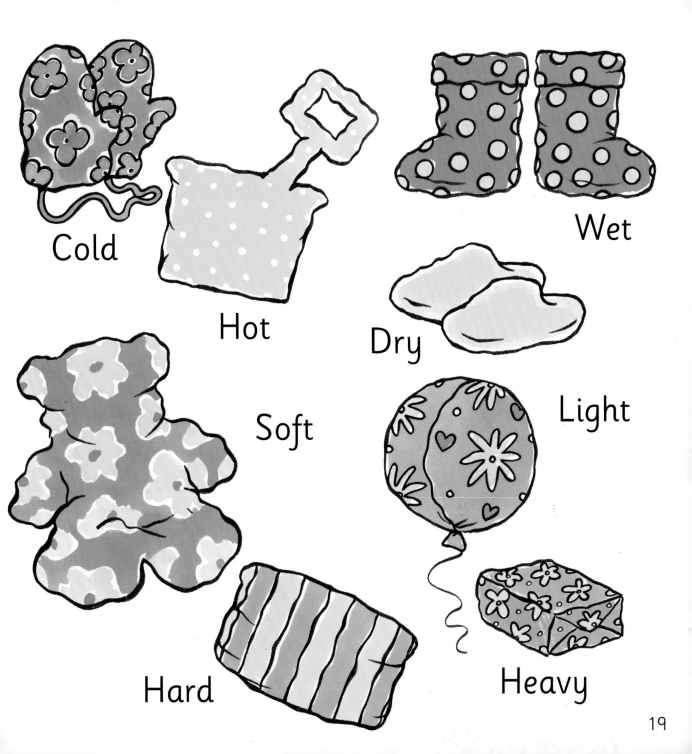

Cold

Hot

Wet

Dry

Light

Soft

Hard

Heavy

19

Happy Birthday Oscar!

21

22

23

beginner bees

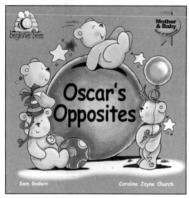

Charlie's Colours
Hb ISBN: 07500 2837 8
Pb ISBN: 07500 2841 6

Buzzy Bee's 123
Hb ISBN: 07500 2835 1
Pb ISBN: 07500 2839 4

Oscar's Opposites
Hb ISBN: 07500 2836 X
Pb ISBN: 07500 2840 8

What's that Shape?
Hb ISBN: 07500 2838 6
Pb ISBN: 07500 2842 4

All these books and many more can be purchased from your local bookseller. For more information, write to:

The Sales Department, Macdonald Young Books, 61 Western Road, Hove BN3 1JD